A Taste of the Wild

A Taste of the Wild

Cooking with the Good Things From Nature's Garden

With Recipes by Jack Tobin,
Host of Radio's
"Let's Get Growing!"

Illustrated by
Merrily Johnson

♔
Hallmark Editions

Country Greens
1 qt. each dandelion
and spinach greens
1/2 c. butter
1/4 c. soft ch
(over)

Salt

"Walk on the Wild Side!"

Even in the age of concrete and super highways, Americans can still live off the land. In A Taste of the Wild you'll learn that plants long considered "pests" can actually add to your larder.

Some, such as the morel mushroom or wild strawberry, stand alone as gourmet treats. And, they abound in the woods and pastures around us!

Find a fallen elm in the forest, and weather conditions being right, some spring you'll harvest morels in abundance. Once you've tasted them, you'll treasure your secret mushroom patch forever!

Now my family is composed of five avid fishermen. Whenever possible we weekend at the lake. Once, with the fishing good but the catching poor, we decided to hunt wild strawberries. My thirteen- and fourteen-year-old sons wanted no part of hunting. They'd come to fish!

Parental authority won out, however, and hunting we went.

We found one particular sunny hillside which was literally covered with berries. In about fifteen minutes after tasting these fantastic little wonders, my boys were confirmed berry hunters. That evening we had "Wild Strawberry Crepes." Today, when spring and the berries arrive, we have trouble getting the boys in the boat!

Remember, the recipes in this book are not designed to act as a "survival kit." They are meant to give you an appreciation of many wild plants that are really much more than pests and weeds.

Take pokeweed as just one example. Close your eyes and you'd swear it's the finest asparagus you've ever tasted! The greens add a touch that can't be found in "tame" plants.

Many of the wild plants in <u>A Taste of the Wild</u> were staples in the diet of

American Indians. Others, like sassafras, were among the first American exports to the old world. It is sad, in a way, that so much natural abundance has been neglected in recent years.

Last but not least, you'll find that hunting the herbs and plants of our woods and meadows will do more for you than the eating. You'll have an opportunity to see God's wonders, not through the haze of a city's smog, but through the clean crisp air of His outdoors.

The flowers and wild plants in these recipes are easily found throughout the United States--many like wild onion and nutgrass in your own backyard. So whether you're a suburbanite, a city dweller, or a lifelong resident of Possum Corner, get outside for good eating! Please accept my personal invitation to "walk on the wild side."

Sincerely yours,
Jack Tobin

Cress Canapé
An Outdoor Hors d'oeuvre!

1¼ cups watercress
6 oz. cream cheese
1 tbsp. lemon juice
½ tsp. Worcestershire sauce
2 tbsp. french dressing
¼ tsp. dry mustard
2 tbsp. chopped ripe olives

Wash watercress thoroughly. Dry and chop fine. Mix all ingredients together. Spread on favorite cracker or bread sautéd in butter.

Watercress

This native of gravelly, gently flowing brooks is a natural storehouse of valuable minerals and vitamins B, C, and E.

Wild Onion

Aroma is a sure clue to the location of this lawn "pest," a diminutive cousin of the commercial onion. Its smell is unmistakably "onion."

Wild Onion Soup

2 cups wild onions or 3 cups leeks
1 qt. beef bouillon
1 tsp. Worcestershire sauce
½ tsp. salt
⅛ tsp. cracked pepper

Wash onions or leeks and slice thin. Cover with water in a saucepan and boil 2 minutes. Drain.

Melt 3 tbsp. butter in small skillet. Sauté drained onions.

Combine all ingredients in a saucepan. Bring to a boil. Place in soup tureen or individual bowls. Garnish with small slice of french bread that has been sprinkled with grated Parmesan cheese and broiled until cheese has melted.

Wild, Wild Salad

Salad:
- 1 cup chickweed
- 1 cup dandelion greens
- 2 cups raw spinach
- 3 sliced green onions and tops
- 3 chopped hard-cooked eggs

Dressing:
- 8 slices bacon, cooked and crumbled
- 1/3 cup bacon fat
- 1/3 cup white vinegar
- 1 1/2 tsp. dry mustard
- 1 1/2 tsp. garlic salt
- 1/2 tsp. salt
- 1 tsp. pepper

Wash and dry leaves thoroughly. Chill in refrigerator.

Bring dressing ingredients to a boil. Pour over chilled greens, coating leaves thoroughly. Sprinkle chopped eggs over top. Serve fresh.

Chickweed

This "plague" of lawn and garden is, in fact, a valuable foodstuff rich in iron.

Dandelion

Everyone knows the
dandelion, the flower
that brings sunshine to
fields and meadows
everywhere.

Country Greens

1 qt. each dandelion and spinach greens
½ cup butter
¼ cup soft bread cubes
2 finely chopped hard-cooked eggs
1 tbsp. chopped watercress
  Salt and pepper to taste

Wash greens in warm water, then in cold running water. Plunge dandelions into boiling water. Cook 5 minutes. Drain. Add ½ cup water and spinach. Cook 10-12 minutes until tender. Do not overcook. Add 2 tbsp. butter and salt and pepper.

In skillet, melt ½ cup butter. When butter foams, add bread cubes. Cook over low heat until brown. Remove from heat and stir in eggs, watercress, and salt and pepper to taste. Pour over hot greens.

Batter-Fried Morel Mushrooms

Slice mushrooms lengthwise and soak in cold, salted water 2 or 3 hours. Drain and wash each one under cold running water.

Prepare a batter (medium thin) of egg, milk and flour. Dip each piece of morel in batter and fry until golden brown and crisp. There are three choices for frying, and each is so durned good, I still can't decide which is best:

Deep, hot vegetable oil
Butter
Half bacon fat, half oil

Find that treasure spot where the morels grow, prepare them as the recipe calls for, and you'll become as avid a mushroom hunter as I am!

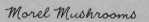

Morel Mushrooms

From March to May mushroom hunters will find the spongelike morel in apple orchards, open woods, and frequently on the grassy banks of streams.

Nasturtium

Considered a gourmet
delicacy in times past,
the lovely nasturtium is
cultivated in gardens
across the country.

Nasturtium Salad Dressing

½ cup olive oil
½ cup red wine vinegar
1 tsp. salt
¼ tsp. freshly ground pepper
1 clove garlic
1 tbsp. chopped onion
1 small piece hot red pepper
2 cups clean nasturtium flowers

Combine all ingredients in quart jar, seal tightly and shake well. Let stand 2 weeks. Remove garlic and flowers.

Pokeweed au Gratin

1½ lbs. pokeweed shoots
⅓ cup slivered almonds
3 tbsp. butter
4 tbsp. grated Parmesan cheese
   Salt and pepper to taste

Gather young pokeweed shoots when 3-4 inches tall. Strip leaves and wash sprouts in cold water.

Boil 2 minutes. Drain and add fresh water. Boil until tender.

Place in buttered casserole, salt and pepper to taste. Sprinkle with slivered almonds, butter and cheese. Place under broiler until lightly browned and cheese is melted.

Pokeweed

The roots and berries of
this plant are poisonous.
However, the young
shoots (before the crimson
color appears) are
harmless and tasty.

Milkweed

Gather the pods of this
backyard compost native
in the early morning
when they are most
tender.

Batter-Fried Milkweed Pods

Milkweed pods
1 egg
1 tbsp. water
Cracker crumbs
2 tbsp. butter
3 tbsp. vegetable oil
Salt and pepper to taste

Find young, firm milkweed pods. Wash well. Cover with water and boil 3 minutes. Drain.

Beat egg with a fork and add water. Dip pod in batter and roll in finely crushed cracker crumbs. Fry in hot mixture of vegetable oil and butter.

Wild Rice

Late summer is
harvesttime for wild
rice, the Indian favorite
found in still ponds.

Wild Rice

1 cup raw wild rice
¼ cup diced salt pork
⅓ cup diced onion
½ cup chopped celery
½ tsp. salt
¼ tsp. sage
⅛ tsp. thyme
⅛ tsp. black pepper
4 tbsp. butter

Sauté onion, celery and salt pork in 2 tbsp. butter. Add spices.

In saucepan, bring 3 cups water to a boil. Add sautéd mixture and rice. Simmer 1 ½ hours or until rice is soft. Add 2 tbsp. butter and more salt and pepper if needed.

Excellent with game and fowl, topped with a cream gravy.

Day Lily Zucchini

½ cup buds and blossoms of day lilies
1½ – 2 lbs. zucchini
3 tbsp. butter
Salt and pepper to taste

Wash and towel dry lilies and zucchini.
Remove stem ends and slice zucchini.

Melt butter in skillet. Add lilies and
zucchini and cook gently until tender
(about 8–10 minutes). Do not overcook.
The zucchini should not be mushy.

Day lily zucchini makes a tasty, attractive
change from ho-hum vegetables.

Day Lily

Fragrant day lilies add a delightful orange and yellow accent to backyards, roadsides, and meadows.

Wood Sorrel

Rich in vitamin C,
sorrel is fond of the
shady places around
stone walls and home
foundations. It is a
small, delicate plant
about seven inches tall
with light green clover-
shaped leaves.

Chicken Sorrel

4-5 lb. stewing hen
⅓ cup diced celery
2 chicken bouillon cubes
2 tsp. salt
⅓ tsp. pepper
½ cup sorrel, washed and finely shredded
6 small new potatoes
1 pkg. frozen peas
¼ cup cornstarch

Cut hen in serving pieces. Place in large kettle. Cover with water. Add all ingredients except potatoes and peas.

Bring to a boil. Reduce heat and simmer 2-2½ hours or until chicken is tender.

Remove chicken from kettle and bone. Add potatoes to broth and cook until almost done. Add peas and boned chicken and cook 5-8 minutes. Thicken with ¼ cup cornstarch blended with cold milk until smooth.

Wild Plantain Stuffing

¾ cup chopped wild onion
¾ cup finely chopped celery
¾ cup butter
1 bunch finely chopped watercress
1 bunch finely chopped plantain
¾ cup breadcrumbs
  Sage (optional)
  Salt and pepper to taste

Sauté onion and celery in half the butter.
Add the watercress and plantain. Season
to taste.

Cook until all liquids evaporate. Melt
remaining butter, stir in breadcrumbs
and add to watercress and plantain
mixture.

A savory dressing excellent with any fowl!

Plantain

Easily recognized by its tall spire of seeds, plantain can be found all over the countryside as well as on the streets of a big city.

Ham and Potatoes With Peppergrass

14 boiled new potatoes
2 cups cubed, cooked ham
6 slices bacon
½ cup sliced green onion
¾ tsp. finely chopped peppergrass
2 tbsp. chopped green pepper
1 tsp. dry mustard
1 tsp. salt
¼ tsp. pepper
3 tbsp. vinegar
½ cup water
1 cup mayonnaise
⅓ cup chopped sweet pickle

Cook bacon until crisp. Remove and crumble.
Add onion and green pepper to bacon fat and sauté until soft. Blend in mayonnaise, salt, pepper, mustard and peppergrass. Add water and vinegar. Cook and stir until bubbly. Fold in chopped pickle and pour over potatoes and ham. Sprinkle with bacon bits.

Peppergrass

Another lawn "pest,"
peppergrass thrives in
dry, sandy soils and
was used formerly by
seamen as a cure for
scurvy.

Juniper Berries

Hunting for juniper
berries among dry hills
and limestone areas is
a pleasant pastime for
September afternoons.

Juniper Quail

8 quail or 2 pheasant cut in serving pieces
⅔ cup melted butter
   Paprika
3 tbsp. chopped onion
3 tbsp. chopped celery
⅓ cup diced carrots
1 beef bouillon cube
1 cup boiling water
1 pinch thyme
1 cup dry white wine
¾ cup juniper berries

Sauté vegetables in 2 tbsp. of butter until soft. Add all ingredients except butter and paprika.

Baste birds with butter. Sprinkle generously with paprika. Place under broiler until golden brown. Place in buttered casserole. Add sauce and bake at 350° for 35-45 minutes depending on size of birds.

Sassafras

Sassafras, the "wild
cinnamon" of our shady
woods, finds its way into
many native American
recipes.

Sassafras Tea

Scrub small sassafras roots carefully. Place handful in boiling water for 3-5 minutes or until water turns red. Sweeten with cream and sugar.

Grandma used to say that this was a great spring tonic!

Nutgrass Biscuits

1½ cups sifted white flour	1 tsp. salt
½ cup nutgrass flour	¼ cup shortening
1 tbsp. baking powder	¾ cup milk

Dig nutgrass and cut the tubers or "nuts" from the roots and base of plant. Wash and dry. Place on cookie sheet and dry in slow oven with door ajar for several hours. When nut can be broken with a sharp blow, it is dry enough to put in blender. Blend to fine flour.

In bowl, mix flour, nutgrass flour, baking powder and salt. Blend thoroughly.

Use a pastry blender or knife and fork to cut in shortening. Blend until mixture resembles cornmeal.

Add milk and mix until all ingredients are moistened.

Knead on floured surface 15-20 strokes. Roll dough ½ inch thick. Cut with biscuit cutter. Place on ungreased cookie sheet. Bake at 450° for 12-15 minutes.

Nutgrass

Harvested both in fall and spring, nutgrass grows naturally in any rich, damp soil.

FLOUR

Persimmon

Popular in colonial days, the persimmon tree survives now as an old, respected resident of many backyards and forests.

Early American Persimmon Cake

Cake:
1 pkg. yellow cake mix
1 cup strained persimmon pulp

Icing:
½ cup soft butter
3½ cups sifted confectioners' sugar
1 pinch salt
¼–⅓ cup strained persimmon pulp
½ tsp. vanilla extract

Be sure persimmons are ripe. They should be soft and a little wrinkled. At this point, the stem will slip out easily and the persimmons will be sweet.

Follow instructions on cake mix box. Fold in persimmon pulp.
Cream together butter, sugar, salt, vanilla extract, and more persimmon pulp for a delightful persimmon icing. Mix until creamy and of spreading consistency. If too thick, add a few drops of cream.

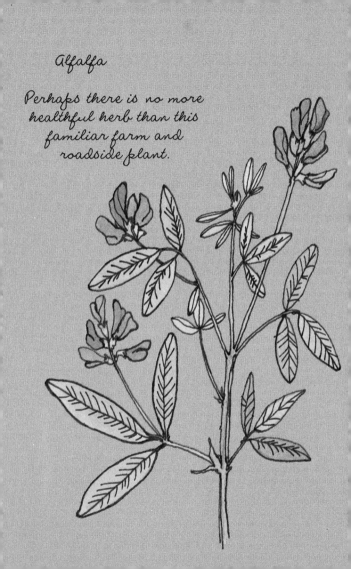

Alfalfa

Perhaps there is no more
healthful herb than this
familiar farm and
roadside plant.

Alfalfa Tea

Simply select clean alfalfa seed. The only important thing to remember is that the water should not boil. Steep the seed until the desired strength is reached. Sweeten with honey for a delicious, nutritious drink. Vitamin rich alfalfa tea also mixes well with fruit juices and soups.

Sugar Rose Petals and Violet Flowers

Beaten egg white
Fine granulated sugar
(colored if you like)

Pick perfect rose petals and violets. Dip in beaten egg white. Place on paper towel and sprinkle generously with sugar. Dry in warm spot.

After drying, repeat procedure.

Natural sugar roses make beautiful decorations for all kinds of desserts. They look good, and they taste the same way.

Roses

Few people know that America's favorite flower is also a flavorful food.

Wild
Strawberry

Summer finds the wild
strawberry ripening in
dry soil and open fields.

Wild Strawberry Crepes

Crepes:
- 2 cups flour
- 1 tsp. sugar
- 1 pinch salt
- 5 eggs
- 1½ cups milk
- 4 tbsp. heavy cream
- 2 tbsp. melted butter

Filling:
- 1 qt. wild strawberries (sweeten to taste)
- 3 oz. cream cheese
- ⅔ cup whipping cream
- ⅛ tsp. almond extract

Sift flour, sugar, and salt in large bowl. Blend eggs with fork. <u>Do not beat.</u> Add to flour and stir until smooth. Gradually add milk, cream and melted butter. Heat small skillet. Add ½ tsp. butter. When bubbly, pour in small amount of batter. Tilt pan immediately so batter covers bottom. Brown lightly on both sides. Place between paper towels to keep warm. Mash cream cheese and almond extract. Add cream, beat until thick and creamy. Fold in strawberries. Place 3 tbsp. on each crepe and roll. Top with sweetened whipped cream and a whole strawberry.

Jack Tobin

Raised in the rural Midwest, Jack Tobin brings some fifty years experience of the outdoors to A Taste of the Wild, his guide to the abundance of nature's pantry.

First as a seed and grain dealer, then as a newspaper columnist, radio and television personality, Jack has lent his expertise to countless thousands of avid gardeners, horticulturists, and lawn-proud suburbanites. His message in A Taste of the Wild is strikingly simple— "There is an herb garden at your feet, a green grocery in your own backyard!"

Some of the recipes in this book were contributed by Jack's many friends in his radio-television audience. Others are kitchen traditions from grandmother's day, an age when living off the land was second nature. As Jack says, "They're all so durned good, I can't make up my mind which I like best!"